Night Light

Written by:
William & Rebecca Lehman

Art by:
Thomas Lamkin Jr.

This book is a work of fiction. Names, characters, and incidents are a product of the author's imagination or are used fictitiously. Any resemblance to any persons, living or dead, is entirely coincidental.

Copyright ©2026 Line By Lion Publications
www.pixelandpen.studio
ISBN 979-8-9988123-1-6

Illustrations by: Thomas Lamkin Jr.

All rights reserved. In accordance with the U.S. Copyright Act of 1976, the scanning, uploading, and electronic sharing of any part of this book without the permission of the author is unlawful piracy and the theft of the author's intellectual property. If you would like to use material from the book (other than for review purposes), prior written permission must be obtained by contacting the publisher. Thank you for respecting author rights.

NO AI TRAINING: Without in any way limiting the author's [and publisher's] exclusive rights under copyright, any use of this publication to "train" generative artificial intelligence (AI) technologies to generate text is expressly prohibited. The author reserves all rights to license uses of this work for generative AI training and development of machine learning language models. Furthermore, Line By Lion Publications affirms that NO AI is used in the creation of our art. Support real artists!

To the adopted children in our lives - Be the light for those still finding their way.

You should never fear what's in the dark
For there is a secret I must impart
When it's time to say goodnight
There are those afraid of the light

When the sun is up they stay out of sight
All while wondering what's in the light
They dare not peek until the sun is down
Afraid of noises bright and loud

There are snowy owls that sleep all day
But at night come out to play
They fly and sing their hooting "whooos"
All while being afraid of you

And raccoons you will not see in the sun
It is at night they have their fun
They'll run and hide when you're around
Up a tree or on the ground

Possums look quite silly in the light
In fact it gives them such a fright
They'll lay down and there they'll stay
Until the light all goes away

Porcupines are quite prickly

And skunks are notoriously stinky

But both will stay hidden out of sight

Until you are in your bed at night

There are some frogs who only play
When it's dark at end of day
They are afraid of children you see
Who like to catch them in their trees

Fireflies are quite lovely to behold
But they can not shine in light so bold
They sleep all day until the sun goes down
And then they glow all around

These creatures are quite nice you see
Though not at all like you and me
It is at night they eat and play
And go to bed at break of day

So do not fret when it is dark

Now you can see it plays its part

For these animals who are afraid of light

Are all quite thankful for the night

About the Illustrator

Thomas Lamkin Junior was born in White Sands, Arizona. The eldest son of a preacher an an educator, he had an idyllic childhood before graduating from University of North Carolina, Wilmington, and returning to Louisville, Kentucky to spend time with his ageing grandmother. Thomas met his wife, Amanda, an a fandom expo on a day in which he'd decided that it was time to take a break from his introversion. He has since raised their children as his own on their shared farm full of useless but enjoyable misfit animals. An avid Tolkein fan, Thomas admires Samwise, adores Gandalf, but freely acknowledges he's mostly Treebeard.

About the Authors

William Lehman grew up in central Ohio with a stack of books always nearby and a pen never far from his hand. He wrote letters to his favorite authors as a kid. (A few even wrote back!) In adulthood, he's never stopped chasing stories. A creator at heart, he's tried everything from airbrushing and painting, to photography and woodworking. These days, you'll often find him bringing stories to life in the wood shop, or streaming as a content creator on Twitch.

Rebecca Lehman grew up moving all across Kentucky. Wherever she landed, her books always came with her. She studied Art Education in college before realizing her true passion was in creating rather than teaching. In her spare time, she still writes poetry and sketches. She can often be found exploring the quiet corners of the forest. (possibly trying to befriend the creatures there, but that's not crazy or anything) Her deep love of detail and wonder finds its way into both her art and her writing.

The two met in an online chatroom, married in 2005, and now raise three children—each with a literary name. Their early years started off working together in fulltime ministry, now they run a woodworking business, traveling to Renaissance faires where they sell their creations. Everything they do—whether crafting with wood, writing stories, or even venturing to the local coffee shop—is rooted in a shared love of adventure and storytelling.

They draw inspiration from authors like Stephen Lawhead and C.S. Lewis, and their faith shapes the heart of their writing. For both William and Rebecca, books were lifelines during difficult childhood seasons, offering adventure and hope in dark times. Now, their own stories aim to do the same: to remind readers that the destination is just as important as the journey, and even in the storm there can be light.

To quote another of their favorite authors: "Those of us who write, who sing, who paint, must remember that to a child a song may glow like a nightlight in a scary bedroom... it is the sword we swing in the Kingdom, to remind children that the good guys win, that the stories are true, and that a fool's hope may be the best kind."

-paraphrased from Adorning the Dark, by Andrew Peterson

Rebecca would especially like to thank her parents for planting the seeds for a love of stories early on—through trips to the library, gifts of books and art supplies, and pushing her to keep writing, even on days she didn't want to, and her diary entries were titled, "I'm writing this because I have to."

www.ingramcontent.com/pod-product-compliance
Lightning Source LLC
Chambersburg PA
CBHW041915230426
43673CB00016B/417